READ-ALOUD RHYMES FOR THE VERY YOUNG

READ-ALOUD
RHYMES
FOR THE VERY YOUNG

SELECTED BY

JACK PRELUTSKY

ILLUSTRATED BY

MARC BROWN

With an Introduction by

JIM TRELEASE

ALFRED A. KNOPF 🐕 NEW YORK

THIS IS A BORZOI BOOK PUBLISHED BY
ALFRED A. KNOPF, INC.

Copyright © 1986 by Alfred A. Knopf, Inc.
Illustrations copyright © 1986 by Marc Brown.
Introduction copyright © 1986 by Jim Trelease.
All rights reserved under International
and Pan-American Copyright Conventions.
Published in the United States by Alfred A. Knopf, Inc.,
New York, and simultaneously in Canada by Random House
of Canada Limited, Toronto. Distributed by
Random House, Inc., New York.
Manufactured in the United States of America

BOOK DESIGN BY DENISE CRONIN

9   10

Library of Congress Cataloging-in-Publication Data

Read-aloud rhymes for the very young.

Summary: A collection of more than 200
short poems by both known and anonymous
American and English authors.
1. Children's poetry, American. 2. Children's poetry, English.
3. Nursery rhymes.
[1. American poetry—Collections.
2. English poetry—Collections]
I. Prelutsky, Jack. II. Brown, Marc Tolon, ill.
PS586.3.R4 1986   811'.008'09282   86-7147
ISBN 0-394-87218-5
ISBN 0-394-97218-X (lib. bdg.)

For Janet Schulman
—J.P.

Drawn with love for Eliza Morgan Brown
—M.B.

🔲 INTRODUCTION 🔲

EVERYONE is aware that children are great *asking machines*. Indeed, research shows us that children ask about thirty questions an hour: Who? What? When? Where? Why? And with good reason, for these questions are the principal tools children use to discover and understand the world around them.

However, most adults forget that long before children become great asking machines, they are great *listening machines*. The newborn infant is a marvelously discerning listener, always reacting to a woman's voice instead of a man's when both speak simultaneously. And why not? He's been listening almost exclusively to the frequency of a woman's voice for the last nine months. Within ten weeks after birth this acuity has grown to the point where the average baby can pick out his mother's voice from all others. Pretty sharp listener for such a little person, wouldn't you say?

The relevance of all this to a collection of poetry is demonstrated by the fact that the first sound a child hears is actually a poem—the rhythmic, rhyming beat-beat-beat of a mother's heart. This early and fundamental relationship sets the stage for a natural and lifelong love of rhythm and rhyme. It's demonstrated by the ease with which young children learn anything set to music, such as TV commercials, the way they are lulled to sleep by the repetitious purr of a motor, and their tendency to sing or hum songs when they are happy. And songs are, after all, nothing more than poetry set to music.

No one better recognizes the essence of the child-poetry connection than poet and anthologist Jack Prelutsky. What he accomplished for older children in *The Random House Book of Poetry*, he has duplicated for younger children in *Read-Aloud Rhymes for the Very Young*. Here are more than two hundred little poems to feed little people with little attention spans to help both grow. Marc Brown's inviting illustrations add a visual dimension to the poems, which further engage young imaginations.

Children have a near-genius capacity to absorb and process language between twelve months and six years of age, learning an average of nine new words a day. Research further shows us that the richer and more plentiful the language environment, the richer will be the child's vocabulary. The child will learn to read more easily, and will have fewer learning difficulties. Simply put, if the child has never *heard* the word, the child will never *say* the word; and if you have neither heard it nor said it, it's pretty tough to *read* it and to *write* it.

Next to hugging and talking to children, reading aloud is the greatest gift we can give them. Beyond the positive role modeling and physical bonding taking place, we are stimulating imagination, enriching vocabulary, building listening skills, and whetting the appetite for a love of reading.

Over the years we have discovered a pattern in *which* words children learn. They choose first those words with some personal meaning—Mommy, Daddy, Nana, milk, cup, potty, dog, water, shoe, etc. This pattern continues right into adult life. The poets included in this collection know this instinctively. They use words that relate to what children see and feel every day. So you'll find words here about bedtime, moon and stars, about mornings, noses, and sneezes. They know little people are naturally interested by little things: mittens, butterflies, chicks, crumbs, snowflakes, kittens, mice, caterpillars, and ants. And thus they populate their poetry with them. They also know that children's imaginations gravitate to nonsense and wonder, music and thunder; therefore they also write about elves and fairies, shadows and dragons. As the vocabulary grows, so too does comprehension and attention span.

"Read it again!" is a child's version of "Bravo! Encore, maestro!" The brevity of these poems allows the reader to be generous with encores.

The poets represented in this volume have not forgotten what it was like to be three years old. Frances Frost's poem "Squirrel in the Rain" magically transported me back thirty-five years to an apartment house window where I spent many winter hours pondering the fate and living quarters of tiny gray squirrels across the street. Reading such poems aloud allows us to visit with the child within each of us, and each visit gives us a better understanding of the child on our lap or in our classroom.

Unlike the toys we buy our children, poems cannot break. Their flavor will last longer than a hundred boxes of candy. They come already assembled and need only one battery—a reader connected to one child. And that reader can start a glow that lasts a lifetime.

JIM TRELEASE
Springfield, Massachusetts
May 1986

SINGING-TIME

I wake in the morning early
And always, the very first thing,
I poke out my head and I sit up in bed
And I sing and I sing and I sing.

Rose Fyleman

THE RAGGEDY DOG

The Raggedy Dog chased the Raggedy Cat
　　And she climbed to the top of a tree;
So the Raggedy Dog came a-running and sat
　　Underneath until quarter-past three.

That night as the moon rose over the hill
　　And the Raggedy Man came around,
The Cat lay asleep in the branches so still,
　　And the Dog was asleep on the ground.

Sherman Ripley

THE SNAIL AND THE MOUSE

The Snail and the Mouse
Went round the house,
　　Running a race together;
The riders were elves,
And proud of themselves,
　　For neither weighed more than a feather.

The Snail went crawly, creepy, crawl,
　　The Mouse went hoppety hop, sir;
But they came to a fence
That *was* so immense
　　(Six inches!), they *had* to stop, sir!

Laura E. Richards

A FROG AND A FLEA

A frog and a flea
And a kangaroo
Once jumped for a prize
In a pot of glue;
The kangaroo stuck
And so did the flea,
And the frog limped home
With a fractured knee.

Cynthia Mitchell

4

HIGGLETY, PIGGLETY, POP!

Higglety, pigglety, pop!
The dog has eaten the mop;
    The pig's in a hurry,
    The cat's in a flurry,
Higglety, pigglety, pop!

Samuel Goodrich

RUN A LITTLE

Run a little this way,
    Run a little that!
Fine new feathers
    For a fine new hat.
A fine new hat
    For a lady fair–
Run round and turn about
    And jump in the air.

Run a little this way,
    Run a little that!
White silk ribbon
    For a black silk cat.
A black silk cat
    For the Lord Mayor's wife–
Run around and turn about
    And fly for your life!

James Reeves

5

JUST WATCH

Watch
   how high
   I'm jumping,

Watch
   how far
   I hop,

Watch
   how long
   I'm skipping,

   Watch
     how fast
     I stop!

Myra Cohn Livingston

WHISTLING

Oh, I can laugh and I can sing
and I can scream and shout,
but when I try to whistle,
the whistle won't come out.

I shape my lips the proper way,
I make them small and round,
but when I blow, just air comes out,
there is no whistling sound.

But I'll keep trying very hard
to whistle loud and clear,
and someday soon I'll whistle tunes
for everyone to hear.

Jack Prelutsky

6

JUMP OR JIGGLE

Frogs jump
Caterpillars hump

Worms wiggle
Bugs jiggle

Rabbits hop
Horses clop

Snakes slide
Sea gulls glide

Mice creep
Deer leap

Puppies bounce
Kittens pounce

Lions stalk—
But—
I walk!

Evelyn Beyer

HIDE AND SEEK

When I am alone, and quite alone,
I play a game, and it's all my own.

I hide myself
Behind myself,
And then I try
To find myself.

I hide in the closet,
Where no one can see;
Then I start looking
Around for me.

I hide myself
And look for myself;
There once was a shadow
I took for myself.

I hide in a corner;
I hide in the bed;
And when I come near me
I pull in my head!

A. B. Shiffrin

FOOTNOTE

Isn't it foolish to dash off outside
Before making sure that your shoelace is tied?
How silly you'll look when you trip in the street
And land on your fanny instead of your feet!

Norah Smaridge

SWIMMING

Watch me swim!
I lie down so

And make my hands
And both feet go;

I blow to keep
The water away;

And breathe with ease
In the proper way.

I can swim fine
As fine can be

So long as I
Keep out of the sea.

Alice Higgins

DANGEROUS

When we're
Hunting
We explore
Squares upon the
kitchen floor;
We must
Get from
Here   to   there
Without touching
Anywhere;
For this
Square is
Safe for us.
But that one is
Dangerous.

Dorothy Aldis

BLOWING BUBBLES

Dip your pipe and gently blow.
Watch the tiny bubble grow
Big and bigger, round and fat,
Rainbow-colored, and then—
SPLAT!

Margaret Hillert

AN OLD PERSON OF WARE

There was an old person of Ware,
Who rode on the back of a bear:
When they asked, "Does it trot?"
He said, "Certainly not!
He's a Moppsikon Floppsikon bear!"

Edward Lear

POLAR BEAR

The secret of the polar bear
Is that he wears long underwear.

Gail Kredenser

THE ELEPHANT CARRIES A GREAT BIG TRUNK

The elephant carries a great big trunk;
He never packs it with clothes;
It has no lock and it has no key,
But he takes it wherever he goes.

Anonymous

HOLDING HANDS

Elephants walking
Along the trails

   Are holding hands
   By holding tails

Trunks and tails
Are handy things

When elephants walk
In circus rings.

   Elephants work
   And elephants play

   And elephants walk
   And feel so gay.

And when they walk–
It never fails

They're holding hands
By holding tails.

Lenore M. Link

LITTLE WIND

Little wind, blow on the hill-top,
    Little wind, blow down the plain;
Little wind, blow up the sunshine,
    Little wind, blow off the rain.

Kate Greenaway

SHOWERS

Squelch and squirt and squiggle,
Drizzle and drip and drain—
Such a lot of water
Comes down with the rain!

Marchette Chute

THE RAIN

Rain on the green grass,
    And rain on the tree,
And rain on the housetop,
    But not upon me!

Anonymous

RAINY DAY

I do not like a rainy day.
The road is wet, the sky is gray.
They dress me up, from head to toes,
In lots and lots of rubber clothes.
I wish the sun would come and stay.
I do not like a rainy day.

William Wise

MUD

Mud is very nice to feel
All squishy-squash between the toes!
I'd rather wade in wiggly mud
Than smell a yellow rose.

Nobody else but the rosebush knows
How nice mud feels
Between the toes.

Polly Chase Boyden

SUN AFTER RAIN

Rain, rain,
went away.
Sun came out
with pipe of clay,
blew a bubble
whole-world-wide,
stuck a rainbow
on one side.

Norma Farber

13

A SPIKE OF GREEN

When I went out
The sun was hot,
It shone upon
My flower pot.

And there I saw
A spike of green
That no one else
Had ever seen!

On other days
The things I see
Are mostly old
Except for me.

But this green spike
So new and small
Had never yet
Been seen at all!

Barbara Baker

LITTLE SEEDS

Little seeds we sow in spring,
growing while the robins sing,
give us carrots, peas and beans,
tomatoes, pumpkins, squash and greens.

And we pick them,
one and all,
through the summer,
through the fall.

Winter comes, then spring, and then
little seeds we sow again.

Else Holmelund Minarik

HALFWAY DOWN

Halfway down the stairs
Is a stair
Where I sit.
There isn't any
Other stair
Quite like
It.
I'm not at the bottom,
I'm not at the top;
So this is the stair
Where
I always
Stop.

Halfway up the stairs
Isn't up,
And isn't down.
It isn't in the nursery,
It isn't in the town.
And all sorts of funny thoughts
Run round my head:
"It isn't really
Anywhere!
It's somewhere else
Instead!"

A. A. Milne

WILD BEASTS

I will be a lion
    And you shall be a bear,
And each of us will have a den
    Beneath a nursery chair;
And you must growl and growl and growl,
    And I will roar and roar,
And then—why, then—you'll growl again,
    And I will roar some more!

Evaleen Stein

I CAN BE A TIGER

I can't go walking
When they say no,
And I can't go riding
Unless they go.
I can't splash puddles
In my shiny new shoes,
But I can be a tiger
Whenever I choose.

I can't eat peanuts
And I can't eat cake,
I have to go to bed
When they stay awake.
I can't bang windows
And I mustn't tease,
But I can be an elephant
As often as I please.

Mildred Leigh Anderson

17

THE HOUSE CAT

The house cat sits
And smiles and sings.
He knows a lot
Of secret things.

Annette Wynne

CAT KISSES

Sandpaper kisses
on a cheek or a chin—
that is the way
for a day to begin!

Sandpaper kisses—
a cuddle, a purr.
I have an alarm clock
that's covered with fur.

Bobbi Katz

AT NIGHT

When night is dark
my cat is wise
to light the lanterns
in his eyes.

Aileen Fisher

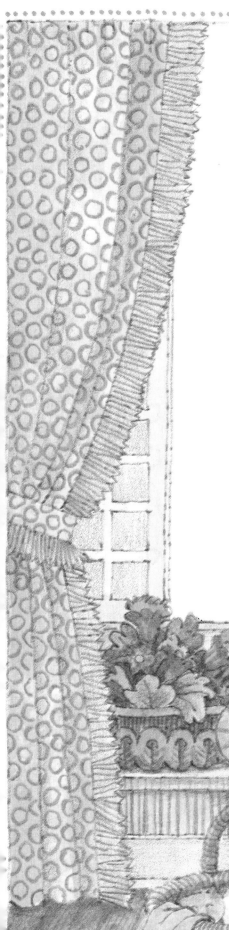

MOTHER CAT'S PURR

Sleep the half-sleep,
Kittens dear,
While your mother
Cat-naps near.

Every kitten
Is a cat,
And you must
Remember that

Naps for cats
Are mostly fake:
Any time
Is time to wake,

Or time to pounce,
Or time to scat.
That's what sleep is—
For a cat.

Jane Yolen

THE LITTLE TURTLE

There was a little turtle.
He lived in a box.
He swam in a puddle.
He climbed on the rocks.

He snapped at a mosquito.
He snapped at a flea.
He snapped at a minnow.
And he snapped at me.

He caught the mosquito.
He caught the flea.
He caught the minnow.
But he didn't catch me.

Vachel Lindsay

A BIG TURTLE

A big turtle sat on the end of a log,
Watching a tadpole turn into a frog.

Anonymous

SNAIL'S PACE

Maybe it's so
that snails are slow.
They trudge along and tarry.

But isn't it true
you'd slow up, too,
if you had a house to carry?

Aileen Fisher

20

The Toad

I met a little woman
who was going up a hill,
and when she wasn't hopping,
she sat extremely still.

She hadn't any neck at all,
she hadn't any chin,
she opened wide her great big mouth
and snapped a young fly in.

She seemed to be good-natured,
and friendly as could be,
for while she swallowed down the fly,
she winked her eye at me.

Elizabeth Coatsworth

The Frog on the Log

There once
Was a green
   Little frog, frog, frog—

Who played
In the wood
   On a log, log, log!

A screech owl
Sitting
   In a tree, tree, tree—

Came after
The frog
   With a scree, scree, scree!

When the frog
Heard the owl—
   In a flash, flash, flash—

He leaped
In the pond
   With a splash, splash, splash!

Ilo Orleans

21

When You Talk to a Monkey

When you talk to a monkey
   He seems very wise.
He scratches his head,
   And he blinks both his eyes;
But he won't say a word.
   He just swings on a rail
And makes a big question mark
   Out of his tail.

Rowena Bennett

Before the Monkey's Cage

The monkey curled his tail about—
   It looked like so much fun
That as I stood and watched him there,
   I wished that I had one.

Edna Becker

MONKEY

HUMMING BIRDS

I think it is a funny thing
That some birds whistle, others sing.
The Warbler warbles in his throat,
The Sparrow only knows one note;
But he is better off than some,
For Humming Birds can only hum.

Betty Sage

SINGING IN THE SPRING

As I was walking along-long-long,
singing a scrap of a song-song-song,
a Blackbird perched in a tree-tree-tree
he whistled my song with me-me-me;
he whistled so sweet and high-high-high
his notes tangled up with the sky-sky-sky!

Ivy O. Eastwick

THE SWALLOW

Swallow, swallow, swooping free,
Do you not remember me?
I think last spring that it was you
Who tumbled down the sooty flue
With wobbly wings and gaping face,
A fledgling in the fireplace.

Remember how I nursed and fed you,
And then into the air I sped you?
How I wish that you would try
To take me with you as you fly.

Ogden Nash

WOODPECKER IN DISGUISE

Woodpecker taps at the apple tree.
"Little bug, open your door," says he.
Little bug says, "Who is it, sir?"
Woodpecker says, "The carpenter."

Grace Taber Hallock

THE OLD WOMAN

You know the old woman
    Who lived in a shoe?
And had so many children
    She didn't know what to do?

I think if she lived in
    A little shoe-house–
That little old woman was
    Surely a mouse!

Beatrix Potter

THE HOUSE MOUSE

Little brown house mouse, laugh and leap,
chitter and cheep while the cat's asleep,
chatter and call and slip through the wall,
trip through the kitchen, skip through the hall.

Little brown house mouse, don't be meek,
dance and squeak and prance and tweak.
There's cheese to take and plenty of cake
as long as you're gone when the cat's awake.

Jack Prelutsky

GOOD NEIGHBORS

A little old woman
    And a little old mouse
Live in the very same
    little old house.
She rocks in a corner,
    He scampers in the wall,
And they never, never get
    in each other's way at all.

May Justus

MICE

I think mice
Are rather nice.

    Their tails are long,
    Their faces small,
    They haven't any
    Chins at all.
    Their ears are pink,
    Their teeth are white,
    They run about
    The house at night.
    They nibble things
    They shouldn't touch
    And no one seems
    To like them much.

But *I* think mice
Are nice.

Rose Fyleman

24

HIDE-AND-SEEK SHADOW

I walked with my shadow,
I ran with my shadow,
I danced with my shadow,
I did.
Then a cloud came over
And the sun went under
And my shadow stopped playing
And hid.

Margaret Hillert

POOR SHADOW

Everything has a shadow—
   A mountain, a bird or a ball—
Only a poor, poor shadow
   Hasn't a shadow at all!

Ilo Orleans

LOOK

Firelight and shadows
dancing on the wall.
Look at my shadow
   TEN FEET TALL!

Charlotte Zolotow

25

BEFORE THE BATH

It's cold, cold, cold,
And the water shines wet,
And the longer I wait
The colder I get.

I can't quite make
Myself hop in
All shivery-cold
In just my skin.

Yet the water's warm
In the tub, I know.
So—one, two, three,
And IN I go!

Corinna Marsh

NAUGHTY SOAP SONG

Just when I'm ready to
Start on my ears,
That is the time that my
Soap disappears.

It jumps from my fingers and
Slithers and slides
Down to the end of the
Tub, where it hides.

And acts in a most diso-
Bedient way
AND THAT'S WHY MY SOAP'S GROWING
THINNER EACH DAY.

Dorothy Aldis

THE WAY THEY SCRUB

The way they scrub
Me in the tub,
I think there's
   Hardly
   Any
   Doubt
Sometime they'll rub
And rub and rub
Until they simply
   Rub
   Me
   Out.

A. B. Ross

WISH

If I could wish,
I'd be a fish
(For just a day or two)
To flip and flash
And dart and splash
And nothing else to do,
And never anyone to say,
"Are you quite sure you washed today?"
I'd like it, wouldn't you?

Dorothy Brown Thompson

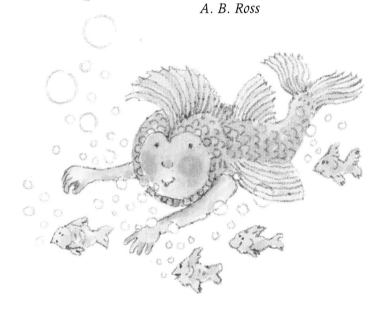

HAPPY WINTER, STEAMY TUB

Happy Winter, steamy tub
To soak and splash in, wash and rub.
Big blobs of bubbles pile on me
The way the snow sits on a tree.
I rinse the soap off, scrub some more,
Drip puddles on the bathroom floor—
Then gurgling bubbles drain away,
A wet and merry end of day.

Karen Gundersheimer

BIG

Now I can catch and throw a ball
And spell
Cat. Dog.
And Pig,
I have finished being small
And started
Being Big.

Dorothy Aldis

SOMETHING ABOUT ME

There's something about me
That I'm knowing.
There's something about me
That isn't showing.

I'm growing!

Anonymous

THE WORLD

The world is big,
And I am small.
The houses all
Are wide and tall.
I run and turn
And trip and fall!

I am so small!
I come and go.
I cannot see,
I cannot know.
I hope it won't
Be always so.

Barbara Young

MY SISTER LAURA

My sister Laura's bigger than me
And lifts me up quite easily.
I can't lift her, I've tried and tried;
She must have something heavy inside.

Spike Milligan

FIVE YEARS OLD

Please, everybody, look at me!
Today I'm *five* years old, you see!
And after this, I won't be four,
Not ever, ever, anymore!
I won't be three—or two—or one,
For that was when I'd first begun.
Now I'll be five a while, and then
I'll soon be something else again!

Marie Louise Allen

THE WISH

Each birthday wish
I've ever made
Really does come true.
Each year I wish
I'll grow some more
And every year
    I
        DO!

Ann Friday

BIRTHDAYS

If birthdays happened once a week
Instead of once a year,
Think of all the gifts you'd get
And all the songs you'd hear
And think how quickly you'd grow up;
Wouldn't it feel queer
If birthdays happened once a week
Instead of once a year?

Mary Ann Hoberman

29

BABY'S BAKING

So, so, spade and hoe,
    Little pile of sand;
See it turning into dough
    In the baby's hand!

Little pie with crimpy crust,
    Set it in the sun;
Sugar it with powdered dust,
    And bake it till it's done.

Evaleen Stein

HOME

The sea is ringed around with hills
And scalloped with white foam;
I've filled my pockets full of shells
And now I'm going home.

Jean Jaszi

SHORE

Play on the seashore
And gather up shells,
Kneel in the damp sands
Digging wells.

Run on the rocks
Where the seaweed slips,
Watch the waves
And the beautiful ships.

Mary Britton Miller

30

WE BUILT A CASTLE NEAR THE ROCKS

We built a castle near the rocks,
  we built it out of sand.

Our fortress was an ice-cream box
  with turret, tall and grand.

Our men were twigs, our guns were straws
  from which we'd sipped at lunch.

We had the very best of wars . . .
  till someone's foot

                went
                    CRUNCH!

Joan Walsh Anglund

THE PICNIC

We brought a rug for sitting on,
Our lunch was in a box.
The sand was warm. We didn't wear
Hats or shoes or socks.

Waves came curling up the beach.
We waded. It was fun.
Our sandwiches were different kinds.
I dropped my jelly one.

Dorothy Aldis

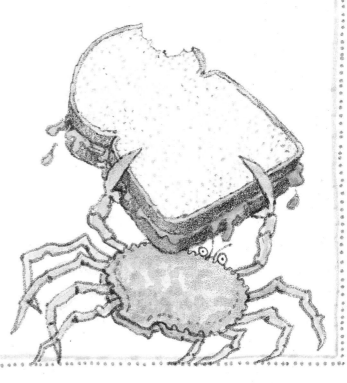

PICNIC DAY

Sing a song of picnics,
    Bread and butter spread,
Greenery all around about,
    And cherries overhead!

           Rachel Field

JOYFUL

A summer day is full of ease,
a bank is full of money,
our lilac bush is full of bees,
and I am full of honey.

           Rose Burgunder

AUGUST HEAT

In August, when the days are hot,
I like to find a shady spot,
And hardly move a single bit—
And sit—
    And sit—
        And sit—
           And sit!

        Anonymous

WOULDN'T YOU?

If I
Could go
As high
And low
As the wind
As the wind
As the wind
Can blow—

I'd go!

John Ciardi

A KITE

I often sit and wish that I
Could be a kite up in the sky,
And ride upon the breeze and go
Whichever way I chanced to blow.

Anonymous

THE BUTTERFLY

Up and down the air you float
Like a little fairy boat;
I should like to sail the sky,
Gliding like a butterfly!

Clinton Scollard

33

THE GOLD-TINTED DRAGON

What's the good of a wagon
Without any dragon
To pull you for mile after mile?
An elegant lean one
A gold-tinted green one
Wearing a dragonly smile.
You'll sweep down the valleys
You'll sail up the hills
Your dragon will shine in the sun
And as you rush by
The people will cry
"I wish that my wagon had one!"

Karla Kuskin

THE TOASTER

A silver-scaled Dragon with jaws flaming red
Sits at my elbow and toasts my bread.
I hand him fat slices, and then, one by one,
He hands them back when he sees they are done.

William Jay Smith

MY DRAGON

I have a purple dragon
With a long brass tail that clangs,
And anyone not nice to me
Soon feels his fiery fangs,

So if you tell me I'm a dope
Or call my muscles jelly,
You just might dwell a billion years
Inside his boiling belly.

X. J. Kennedy

A MODERN DRAGON

A train is a dragon that roars through the dark.
He wriggles his tail as he sends up a spark.
He pierces the night with his one yellow eye,
And all the earth trembles when he rushes by.

Rowena Bennett

35

THE PIGS

Piggie Wig and Piggie Wee,
Hungry pigs as pigs could be,
For their dinner had to wait
Down behind the barnyard gate.

Piggie Wig and Piggie Wee
Climbed the barnyard gate to see,
Peeping through the gate so high,
But no dinner could they spy.

Piggie Wig and Piggie Wee
Got down sad as pigs could be;
But the gate soon opened wide
And they scampered forth outside.

Piggie Wig and Piggie Wee,
What was their delight to see?
Dinner ready not far off—
Such a full and tempting trough!

Piggie Wig and Piggie Wee,
Greedy pigs as pigs could be,
For their dinner ran pell-mell;
In the trough both piggies fell.

Emilie Poulsson

MARY MIDDLING

Mary Middling had a pig,
Not very little and not very big,
Not very pink, not very green,
Not very dirty, not very clean,
Not very good, not very naughty,
Not very humble, not very haughty,
Not very thin, not very fat;
Now what would you give for a pig like that?

Rose Fyleman

THERE WAS A SMALL PIG WHO WEPT TEARS

There was a small pig who wept tears
When his mother said, "I'll wash your ears."
As she poured on the soap,
He cried, "Oh, how I hope
This won't happen again for ten years!"

Arnold Lobel

TEN TO ONE

Ten tired tortoises
lying in the sun;
nine nice neighbors
helping everyone;
eight hasty hostesses
preparing toast for tea;
seven salty sailormen
sailing on the sea;
six savage sharks
all swimming through the deep;
five fluttering fireflies
where the moonbeams peep;
four fat foresters
chopping fine fir trees;
three thin thatchers
a'thatching in the breeze;
two tall tailors
sewing at a seam;
and one wild warrior,
       very wild warrior,
              bow-and-arrow warrior,
eating pink ice-cream.

Ivy O. Eastwick

THE TOP AND THE TIP

Hair is the top of a person,
a chimney's the top of a house,
a cover's the top of a book,
the tail is the tip of a mouse.

The sky is the top of the world,
the top of the sky is space,
a flower's the top of the stem,
the nose is the tip of the face.

Charlotte Zolotow

THE VERY NICEST PLACE

The fish lives in the brook,
The bird lives in the tree,
But home's the very nicest place
For a little child like me.

Anonymous

38

WINGS

Bees have four wings,
birds have two,
I haven't *any*
and that's too few.

Aileen Fisher

MAKERS

Beetlebombs make jelly jam
And bumblebees make honey
Mommy makes the bread and cakes
And Easter eggs make bunnies

Bubbling springs make brooks and things
And rivers make the sea
Grownup frogs make pollywogs
But who made me?

Nancy Dingman Watson

HAPPY THOUGHT

The world is so full of a number of things,
I'm sure we should all be as happy as kings.

Robert Louis Stevenson

THE PUPPY CHASED THE SUNBEAM

The puppy chased the sunbeam
all around the house—
he thought it was a bee,
or a little golden mouse;
he thought it was a spider
on a little silver string;
he thought it was a butterfly
or some such flying thing;
he thought—but oh! I cannot tell you
half the things he thought
as he chased the sparkling sunbeam
which—just—would—not—be—caught.

Ivy O. Eastwick

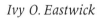

HOW A PUPPY GROWS

I think it's very funny
The way a puppy grows—
A little on his wiggle-tail,
A little on his nose,
A little on his tummy
And a little on his ears;
I guess he'll be a dog all
     right
In half a dozen years.

Leroy F. Jackson

CHUMS

He sits and begs; he gives a paw;
    He is, as you can see,
The finest dog you ever saw,
    And he belongs to me.

He follows everywhere I go
    And even when I swim.
I laugh because he thinks, you know,
    That I belong to him.

Arthur Guiterman

40

SKYSCRAPER

Skyscraper, skyscraper,
Scrape me some sky:
Tickle the sun
While the stars go by.

Tickle the stars
While the sun's climbing high,
Then skyscraper, skyscraper
Scrape me some sky.

Dennis Lee

41

FIVE LITTLE CHICKENS

Said the first little chicken,
  With a queer little squirm,
"I wish I could find
  A fat little worm."

Said the next little chicken,
  With an odd little shrug,
"I wish I could find
  A fat little slug."

Said the third little chicken,
  With a sharp little squeal,
"I wish I could find
  Some nice yellow meal."

Said the fourth little chicken,
  With a small sigh of grief,
"I wish I could find
  A little green leaf."

Said the fifth little chicken,
  With a faint little moan,
"I wish I could find
  A wee gravel stone."

"Now, see here," said the mother,
  From the green garden patch,
"If you want your breakfast,
  Just come here and scratch."

Anonymous

CHOOK, CHOOK

Chook, chook, chook, chook, chook,
  Good morning, Mrs. Hen.
How many chickens have you got?
  Madam, I've got ten.
Four of them are yellow,
  And four of them are brown,
And two of them are speckled red,
  The nicest in the town.

Anonymous

QUACK, QUACK!

We have two ducks. One blue. One black.
And when our blue duck goes "Quack-quack"
our black duck quickly quack-quacks back.
The quacks Blue quacks make her quite a quacker
but Black is a quicker quacker-backer.

Dr. Seuss

A LITTLE TALK

The big brown hen and Mrs. Duck
Went walking out together;
They talked about all sorts of things—
The farmyard, and the weather.
But all *I* heard was:
"Cluck! Cluck! Cluck!"
And "Quack! Quack! Quack!"
from Mrs. Duck.

Anonymous

DUCKS IN THE RAIN

Ducks are dabbling in the rain,
Dibbling, dabbling in the rain.
Drops of water from each back
Scatter as ducks flap and quack.

I can only stand and look
From my window at the brook,
For I cannot flap and quack
And scatter raindrops from my back.

James S. Tippett

FISH

Look at them flit
Lickety-split
Wiggling
Swiggling
Swerving
Curving
Hurrying
Scurrying
Chasing
Racing
Whizzing
Whisking
Flying
Frisking
Tearing around
With a leap and a bound
But none of them making the tiniest
                    tiniest
                tiniest
            tiniest
        sound.

Mary Ann Hoberman

FISH

The little fish are silent
As they swim round and round.
Their mouths are ever talking
A speech without a sound.

Now aren't the fishes funny
To swim in water clear
And talk with words so silent
That nobody can hear?

Arthur S. Bourinot

BELLY & TUBS WENT OUT IN A BOAT

Belly & Tubs went out in a boat,
Tubs wore knickers & Belly a coat,
They got in a quarrel & started to shout
And the boat tipped over & they tumbled out.

Clyde Watson

THE DREADFUL DOINGS OF JELLY BELLY

Jelly Belly bit
    With a big fat bite.
Jelly Belly fought
    With a big fat fight.

Jelly Belly scowled
    With a big fat frown.
Jelly Belly yelled
    Till his house fell down.

Dennis Lee

THE HUNTSMEN

Three jolly gentlemen,
    In coats of red,
Rode their horses
    Up to bed.

Three jolly gentlemen
    Snored till morn,
Their horses champing
    The golden corn.

Three jolly gentlemen,
    At break of day,
Came clitter-clatter down the stairs
    And galloped away.

Walter de la Mare

SLIPPERY SAM

Slippery Sam
Bought a broom,
Ate an apple
And went to the moon;
Swept it clean,
Painted it red,
Came back to earth
And went to bed.

Arnold Spilka

45

TWINKLE, TWINKLE

Twinkle, twinkle, little bat!
How I wonder what you're at!
Up above the world you fly,
Like a tea-tray in the sky.
    Twinkle, twinkle–

Lewis Carroll

THE DONKEY

I had a Donkey, that was all right,
But he always wanted to fly my Kite;
Every time I let him, the String would bust.
Your Donkey is better behaved, I trust.

Theodore Roethke

WAY DOWN SOUTH

Way down South where bananas grow,
A grasshopper stepped on an elephant's toe.
The elephant said, with tears in his eyes,
"Pick on somebody your own size."

Anonymous

46

THERE'S MUSIC IN A HAMMER

There's music in a hammer,
There's music in a nail,
There's music in a pussy cat,
When you step upon her tail.

Anonymous

FUN

I love to hear a lobster
    laugh,
Or see a turtle wiggle,
Or poke a hippopotamus
And see the monster giggle,
Or even stand around at
    night
And watch the mountains
    wriggle.

Leroy F. Jackson

47

THE TOAD AND THE RABBIT

Said the Rabbit to the Hop Toad:
  "It's very strange to me
How very big and long and wide
  A Hop Toad's *mouth* can be."

Said the Hop Toad to the Rabbit:
  "I'm sure I'd shed some tears
If on my head I had to wear
  Such flippy-floppy *ears*."

John Martin

GOOD-MORNING

One day I saw a downy duck,
With feathers on his back;
I said, "Good-morning, downy duck,"
And he said, "Quack, quack, quack."

One day I saw a timid mouse,
He was so shy and meek;
I said, "Good-morning, timid mouse,"
And he said, "Squeak, squeak, squeak."

One day I saw a curly dog,
I met him with a bow;
I said, "Good-morning, curly dog,"
And he said, "Bow-wow-wow."

One day I saw a scarlet bird,
He woke me from my sleep;
I said, "Good-morning, scarlet bird,"
And he said, "Cheep, cheep, cheep."

Muriel Sipe

48

SKELETON PARADE

The skeletons are out tonight,
They march about the street
With bony bodies, bony heads
And bony hands and feet.

Bony bony bony bones
with nothing in between,
Up and down and all around
They march on Halloween.

Jack Prelutsky

ON HALLOWEEN

We mask our faces
and wear strange hats
and moan like witches
and screech like cats
and jump like goblins
and thump like elves
and almost manage
to scare *ourselves.*

Aileen Fisher

BEDTIME STORY

"Tell me a story,"
Says Witch's Child,

"About the Beast
So fierce and wild.

About a Ghost
That shrieks and groans,

A Skeleton
That rattles bones,

About a Monster
Crawly-creepy.

Something nice
To make me sleepy."

Lilian Moore

49

MIX A PANCAKE

Mix a pancake,
Stir a pancake,
Pop it in the pan;
Fry the pancake,
Toss the pancake—
Catch it if you can.

Christina Rossetti

TOASTER TIME

Tick tick tick tick tick tick tick
Toast up a sandwich quick quick quick
Hamwich
Or jamwich
Lick lick lick!

Tick tick tick tick tick tick——stop!
POP!

Eve Merriam

DAVY DUMPLING

Davy Davy Dumpling,
   Boil him in the pot;
Sugar him and butter him,
   And eat him while he's hot.

Anonymous

FIVE LITTLE MONSTERS

Five little monsters
By the light of the moon
Stirring pudding with
A wooden pudding spoon.
The first one says,
"It mustn't be runny."
The second one says,
"That would make it taste funny."
The third one says,
"It mustn't be lumpy."
The fourth one says,
"That would make me grumpy."
The fifth one smiles,
Hums a little tune,
And licks all the drippings
From the wooden pudding spoon.

Eve Merriam

THE WIND AND THE MOON

Said the Wind to the Moon,
"I will blow you out;
    You stare
    In the air
    Like a ghost in a chair
Always looking what I am about.
I hate to be watched—I'll blow you
        out."

George MacDonald

THE MOON'S THE NORTH WIND'S COOKY

The Moon's the North Wind's cooky.
He bites it, day by day,
Until there's but a rim of scraps
That crumble all away.

The South Wind is a baker.
He kneads clouds in his den,
And bakes a crisp new moon *that . . . greedy*
North . . . Wind . . . eats . . . again!

Vachel Lindsay

51

THE MISTLETOE

Mommy,
Daddy,
quick!
Let's go
and stand
beneath
the mistletoe.

You kiss me
and I'll kiss you,
here comes Sister,
kiss her too.

Mommy,
Daddy,
quick!
Let's go
and stand
beneath
the mistletoe.

Jack Prelutsky

DREIDEL SONG

Twirl about, dance about,
   Spin, spin, spin!
Turn, Dreidel, turn—
   Time to begin!

Soon it is Hanukkah—
   Fast, Dreidel, fast!
For you will lie still
   When Hanukkah's past.

Efraim Rosenzweig

DECEMBER

All the months go past
   Each is like a guest;
December is the last,
   December is the best.

Each has lovely things,
   Each one is a friend,
But December brings
   Christmas at the end.

Rose Fyleman

MY TEDDY BEAR

A teddy bear is a faithful friend.
You can pick him up at either end.
His fur is the color of breakfast toast,
And he's always there when you need him most.

Marchette Chute

MY TEDDY BEAR

A teddy bear is nice to hold.
The one I have is getting old.
His paws are almost wearing out
And so's his funny furry snout
From rubbing on my nose of skin,
And all his fur is pretty thin.
A ribbon and a piece of string
Make a sort of necktie thing.
His eyes came out and now instead
He has some new ones made of thread.
I take him everywhere I go
And tell him all the things I know.
I like the way he feels at night,
All snuggled up against me tight.

Margaret Hillert

TEDDY BEAR, TEDDY BEAR

Teddy Bear, Teddy Bear,
Go upstairs.
Teddy Bear, Teddy Bear,
Say your prayers.
Teddy Bear, Teddy Bear,
Turn out the light.
Teddy Bear, Teddy Bear,
Say good night.

Anonymous

53

CATS AND DOGS

Some like cats, and some like dogs,
and both of course are nice
if cats and dogs are what you want
—but I myself like mice.

For dogs chase cats, and cats chase rats
I guess they think it's fun.
I like my mouse the most because
he won't chase anyone.

N. M. Bodecker

JUST THREE

How very quiet things can be,
With just the dog, the cat, and me.
There's no one else to laugh and shout,
To dance and sing and run about.
With just the dog, the cat, and me,
How very quiet things can be.

William Wise

HAMSTERS

Hamsters are the nicest things
That anyone could own.
I like them even better than
Some dogs that I have known.

Their fur is soft, their faces nice.
They're small when they are grown.
And they sit inside your pocket
When you are all alone.

Marci Ridlon

PETER AND WENDY

My ducks are so funny, I think.
    They peck at the bugs in the ground,
And always wherever they go
    They follow each other around.

They like to play Follow the Leader.
    Just watch them awhile and you'll find
There's one of them always in front,
    The other one always behind.

Wymond Garthwaite

UNFORTUNATELY

Dinosaurs lived so long ago,
they never had a chance to know
how many kids would love to get
a dinosaur to be their pet.

Bobbi Katz

ODE TO SPRING

O spring, O spring,
You wonderful thing!
O spring, O spring, O spring!
O spring, O spring,
When the birdies sing
I feel like a king,
    O spring!

Walter R. Brooks

THE SPRING WIND

The summer wind
is soft and sweet
the winter wind is strong
the autumn wind is mischievous
and sweeps the leaves along.

The wind I love the best
comes gently after rain
smelling of spring and growing things
brushing the world with feathery wings
while everything glistens, and everything sings
in the spring wind
after the rain.

Charlotte Zolotow

PUSSY WILLOWS

Close your eyes
and do not peek
and I'll rub Spring
across your cheek—
smooth as satin,
soft and sleek—
close your eyes
and do not peek.

Aileen Fisher

SOME THINGS THAT EASTER BRINGS

Easter duck and Easter chick,
Easter eggs with chocolate thick.

Easter hats for one and all,
Easter Bunny makes a call!

Happy Easter always brings
Such a lot of pleasant things.

Elsie Parrish

THE SQUIRREL

Whisky, frisky
Hippity hop,
Up he goes
To the treetop!

Whirly, twirly,
Round and round,
Down he scampers
To the ground.

Furly, curly,
What a tail!
Tall as a feather,
Broad as a sail!

Where's his supper?
In the shell,
Snappity, crackity,
Out it fell!

Anonymous

GIRAFFES DON'T HUFF

Giraffes don't huff or hoot or howl
They never grump, they never growl
They never roar, they never riot,
They eat green leaves
And just keep quiet.

Karla Kuskin

IN THE SUMMER WE EAT

In the summer we eat,
in the winter we don't;
In the summer we'll play,
in the winter we won't.
All winter we sleep, each curled in a ball
As soon as the snowflakes start to fall.
But in spring we each come out of our de
And start to eat all over again.

Zhenya Gay

58

JOHNNY

To Johnny a box
is a house
or a car
or a ship
or a train
or a horse.
A stick
is a sword
or a spear
or a cane,
and a carpet
is magic,
of course.

Marci Ridlon

YESTERDAY'S PAPER

Yesterday's paper makes a hat,
   Or a boat,
   Or a plane,
   Or a playhouse mat.
Yesterday's paper makes things
   Like that—
   And a very fine tent
   For a sleeping cat.

Mabel Watts

RAINDROPS

How brave a ladybug must be!
Each drop of rain is big as she.

Can you imagine what *you'd* do
if raindrops fell as big as you?

Aileen Fisher

SQUIRREL IN THE RAIN

The young squirrel's mother said, "Come out!
See—it's raining all about!
Wet silver's falling from a cloud!
It's raining hard, it's raining loud!"

The little squirrel ran down the tree:
"It's splashing rain all over *me!*
It's raining here, it's raining there!
It's raining in the trees' green hair,
It's raining in the flowers' faces,
It's raining in the grassy places,
It's raining on my tail and nose
And on my middle, I suppose!
How wonderful of clouds to fly
And give young squirrels a drink of sky!"

Frances Frost

UMBRELLAS

Umbrellas bloom
Along our street
Like flowers on a stem.
And almost everyone
I meet
Is holding one of them.

Under my umbrella-top,
Splashing through the town,
I wonder why the tulips
Hold umbrellas
Up-side-down!

Barbara Juster Esbensen

APRIL

Rain is good
for washing leaves
and stones and bricks and
even eyes,
and if you hold
your head just so
you can almost see
the tops of skies.

Lucille Clifton

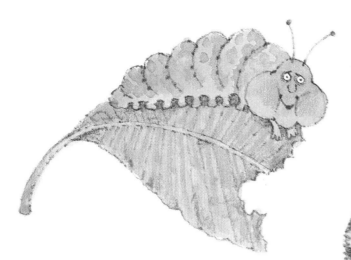

ONLY MY OPINION

Is a caterpillar ticklish?
  Well, it's always my belief
That he giggles, as he wiggles
  Across a hairy leaf.

Monica Shannon

FUZZY WUZZY, CREEPY CRAWLY

Fuzzy wuzzy, creepy crawly
  Caterpillar funny,
You will be a butterfly
  When the days are sunny.

Winging, flinging, dancing, springing
  Butterfly so yellow,
You were once a caterpillar,
  Wiggly, wiggly fellow.

Lillian Schulz

ANTS LIVE HERE

Ants live here
by the curb stone,
      see?
They worry a lot
about giants like
      me.

Lilian Moore

ANTS

I like to watch the ants at work
When I am out at play.
I like to see them run about
And carry crumbs away.

And when I plug an anthill door
To keep them in their den,
I like to see them find a way
To get outside again.

Mary Ann Hoberman

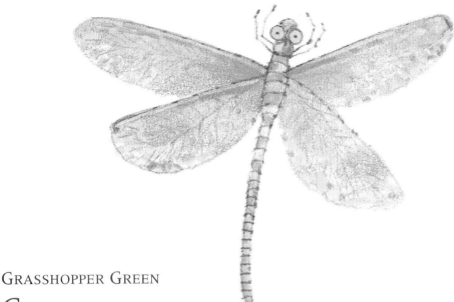

DRAGONFLY

A dragonfly
   Is very thin,
Straight and shining,
   Like a pin,

With narrow wings
   Of stiffened gauze,
And in the air
   He likes to pause

And look at you
   With popping eyes.
He shimmers like
   A small surprise.

Florence Page Jaques

GRASSHOPPER GREEN

Grasshopper green
Too quick to be seen
Jump like a Mexican jumpity bean!

Grasshopper high
Grasshopper low
Over my basket of berries you go!

Grasshopper low
Grasshopper high
Watch it or you will end up in a pie!

Nancy Dingman Watson

BUT I WONDER . . .

The crickets in the thickets,
and the katydids in trees,
and ants on plants, and butterflies,
and ladybugs and bees
don't smell with little noses
but with *feelers,* if you please.
They get along quite nicely,
but I wonder how they *sneeze.*

Aileen Fisher

WHEN ALL THE WORLD'S ASLEEP

Where do insects go at night,
When all the world's asleep?
Where do bugs and butterflies
And caterpillars creep?
Turtles sleep inside their shells;
The robin has her nest.
Rabbits and the sly old fox
Have holes where they can rest.
Bears can crawl inside a cave;
The lion has his den.
Cows can sleep inside the barn,
And pigs can use their pen.
But where do bugs and butterflies
And caterpillars creep,
When everything is dark outside
And all the world's asleep?

Anita E. Posey

NIGHT COMES . . .

Night comes
leaking
out of the sky.

Stars come
peeking.

Moon comes
sneaking,
silvery-sly.

Who is
shaking,
shivery-
quaking?

Who is afraid
of the night?

Not I.

Beatrice Schenk de Regniers

FIREFLY

A little light is going by,
Is going up to see the sky,
A little light with wings.

I never could have thought of it,
To have a little bug all lit
And made to go on wings.

Elizabeth Madox Roberts

SLEEPING OUTDOORS

Under the dark is a star,
Under the star is a tree,
Under the tree is a blanket,
And under the blanket is me.

Marchette Chute

COVERS

Glass covers windows
   to keep the cold away
Clouds cover the sky
   to make a rainy day

Nighttime covers
   all the things that creep
Blankets cover me
   when I'm asleep

Nikki Giovanni

PRETENDING

When you are in bed and it's cold outside,
do you ever pretend that you have to hide?
Do you curl up your toes?
Do you wrinkle your nose?
Do you make yourself little so none of you shows?

Do you pull the sheet over the whole of your face
and pretend you are in some faraway place?
Mother thinks you are sleeping,
but she does not know
that all tucked in your bed, you have places to go.

Bobbi Katz

CRUNCH AND LICK

Popcorn crunches.
Peanuts do.
The cone part of an ice-cream cone
Is wonderful for crunching too.

Things to lick are candy sticks.
Rainbow-colored popsicles.
Chocolate sauce when it begins
To leak and trickle
Down our chins.

Dorothy Aldis

YELLOW BUTTER

Yellow butter purple jelly red jam black bread

Spread it thick
Say it quick

Yellow butter purple jelly red jam black bread

Spread it thicker
Say it quicker

Yellow butter purple jelly red jam black bread

Now repeat it
While you eat it

Yellow butter purple jelly red jam black bread

Don't talk
With your mouth full!

Mary Ann Hoberman

THE MEAL

Timothy Tompkins had turnips and tea.
The turnips were tiny.
He ate at least three.
And then, for dessert,
He had onions and ice.
He liked that so much
That he ordered it twice.
He had two cups of ketchup,
A prune, and a pickle.
"Delicious," said Timothy.
"Well worth a nickel."
He folded his napkin
And hastened to add,
"It's one of the loveliest breakfasts I've had."

Karla Kuskin

TWO SAD

It's such a shock, I almost screech,
    When I find a worm inside my peach!
But then, what *really* makes me blue
    Is to find a worm who's bit in two!

William Cole

TABLE MANNERS

The Goops they lick their fingers,
    And the Goops they lick their knives;
They spill their broth on the tablecloth—
    Oh, they lead disgusting lives!
The Goops they talk while eating,
    And loud and fast they chew;
And that is why I'm glad that I
    Am not a Goop—are you?

Gelett Burgess

TOOTHSOME

No need to squeeze out half a tube
Of toothpaste, honeybunch—
Unless you plan to use it in
a sandwich for your lunch?

Norah Smaridge

69

NIGHT FUN

I hear eating.
I hear drinking.
I hear music.
I hear laughter.
Fun is something
Grownups never have
Before my bedtime.
Only after.

Judith Viorst

BEDTIME

Five minutes, five minutes more, please!
    Let me stay five minutes more!
Can't I just finish the castle
    I'm building here on the floor?
Can't I just finish the story
    I'm reading here in my book?
Can't I just finish this bead-chain—
    It *almost* is finished, look!
Can't I just finish this game, please?
    When a game's once begun
It's a pity never to find out
    Whether you've lost or won.
Can't I just stay five minutes?
    Well, can't I stay just four?
Three minutes, then? two minutes?
    Can't I stay *one* minute more?

Eleanor Farjeon

MOON BOAT

Moon Boat, little, brave and bright,
Tossed upon the seas of night,
One day when I'm free to roam,
I'll climb aboard and steer you home.

Charlotte Pomerantz

I SEE THE MOON

I see the moon,
And the moon sees me;
God bless the moon,
And God bless me.

Anonymous

MOON-COME-OUT

Moon-Come-Out
And Sun-Go-In,
Here's a soft blanket
To cuddle your chin.

Moon-Go-In
And Sun-Come-Out,
Throw off the blanket
And bustle about.

Eleanor Farjeon

THE STAR

Twinkle, twinkle, little star,
How I wonder what you are!
Up above the world so high,
Like a diamond in the sky.

As your bright and tiny spark,
Lights the traveler in the dark—
Though I know not what you are,
Twinkle, twinkle, little star.

Jane Taylor

71

THE LITTLE ELF

I met a little Elf man, once,
  Down where the lilies blow.
I asked him why he was so small,
  And why he didn't grow.

He slightly frowned, and with his eye
  He looked me through and through.
"I'm quite as big for me," said he,
  "As you are big for you."

John Kendrick Bangs

AN EXPLANATION OF THE GRASSHOPPER

The Grasshopper, the Grasshopper,
I will explain to you:
He is the Brownies' racehorse,
The Fairies' Kangaroo.

Vachel Lindsay

FAIRIES

Don't go looking for fairies,
  They'll fly away if you do.
You never can see the fairies
  Till they come looking for you.

Eleanor Farjeon

72

UNDER THE GROUND

What is under the grass,
Way down in the ground,
Where everything is cool and wet
With darkness all around?

Little pink worms live there;
Ants and brown bugs creep
Softly round the stones and rocks
Where roots are pushing deep.

Do they hear us walking
On the grass above their heads;
Hear us running over
While they snuggle in their beds?

Rhoda W. Bacmeister

THE UNDERWORLD

When I am lying in the grass
I watch the ants and beetles pass;
And once I lay so very still
A mole beside me built a hill.

Margaret Lavington

DRAGON SMOKE

Breathe and blow
white clouds
    with every puff.
It's cold today,
    cold enough
to see your breath.
Huff!
   Breathe dragon smoke
    today!

Lilian Moore

THE MORE IT SNOWS

The more it
SNOWS-tiddely-pom,
The more it
GOES-tiddely-pom
The more it
GOES-tiddely-pom
On
Snowing.

And nobody
KNOWS-tiddely-pom,
How cold my
TOES-tiddely-pom
How cold my
TOES-tiddely-pom
Are
Growing.

A. A. Milne

THE MITTEN SONG

"Thumbs in the thumb-place,
Fingers all together!"
This is the song
We sing in mitten-weather.
When it is cold,
It doesn't matter whether
Mittens are wool,
Or made of finest leather—
This is the song
We sing in mitten-weather:
"Thumbs in the thumb-place,
Fingers all together!"

Marie Louise Allen

WINTER SWEETNESS

This little house is sugar.
   Its roof with snow is piled,
And from its tiny window
   Peeps a maple-sugar child.

Langston Hughes

JACK FROST

Someone painted pictures on my
Window pane last night—
Willow trees with trailing boughs
And flowers—frosty white
And lovely crystal butterflies;
But when the morning sun
Touched them with its golden beams,
They vanished one by one!

Helen Bayley Davis

IT FELL IN THE CITY

It fell in the city,
It fell through the night,
And the black rooftops
All turned white.

Red fire hydrants
All turned white.
Blue police cars
All turned white.

Green garbage cans
All turned white.
Gray sidewalks
All turned white.

Yellow NO PARKING signs
All turned white
When it fell in the city
All through the night.

Eve Merriam

75

FIRST SNOW

Snow makes whiteness where it falls.
The bushes look like popcorn-balls.
And places where I always play,
Look like somewhere else today.

Marie Louise Allen

ICY

I slip and I slide
On the slippery ice;
I skid and I glide—
Oh, isn't it nice
To lie on your tummy
And slither and skim
On the slick crust of snow
Where you skid as you swim?

Rhoda W. Bacmeister

JANUARY

In January
it's so nice
while slipping
on the sliding ice
to sip hot chicken soup
with rice.
Sipping once
sipping twice
sipping chicken soup
with rice.

Maurice Sendak

SNOWMAN

My little snowman has a mouth,
So he is always smiling south.
My little snowman has a nose;
I couldn't seem to give him toes,
I couldn't seem to make his ears.
He shed a lot of frozen tears
Before I gave him any eyes—
But they are big ones for his size.

David McCord

SNOW

We'll play in the snow
And stray in the snow
And stay in the snow
In a snow-white park.
We'll clown in the snow
And frown in the snow
Fall down in the snow
Till it's after dark.
We'll cook snow pies
In a big snow pan.
We'll make snow eyes
In a round snow man.
We'll sing snow songs
And chant snow chants
And roll in the snow
In our fat snow pants.
And when it's time to go home to eat
We'll have snow toes
On our frosted feet.

Karla Kuskin

77

IF I WERE BIGGER THAN ANYONE

If I were bigger than anyone,
If I were taller than trees,
I could step over hills and towns
And go anywhere I please.

If I got bored with being huge,
The next day I'd be small.
But the size I really am
I might not choose at all.

Ruth Harnden

OPEN HOUSE

If I were a tree
I'd want to see
a bird with a song
on a branch of me.

I'd want a quick
little squirrel to run
up and down
and around, for fun.

I'd want the cub
of a bear to call,
a porcupine, big,
and a tree-toad, small.

I'd want a katydid
out of sight
on one of my leaves
to sing at night.

And down by my roots
I'd want a mouse
with six little mouselings
in her house.

Aileen Fisher

I'D LIKE TO BE A LIGHTHOUSE

I'd like to be a lighthouse
    All scrubbed and painted white.
I'd like to be a lighthouse
    And stay awake all night
To keep my eye on everything
    That sails my patch of sea;
I'd like to be a lighthouse
    With the ships all watching me.

Rachel Field

TELL ME LITTLE WOODWORM

Tell me little woodworm
Eating through the wood
Surely all that sawdust
Can't do you any good.

Heavens! Little woodworm
You've eaten all the chairs
So *that's* why poor old Grandad's
Sitting outside on the stairs.

Spike Milligan

THREE TICKLES

Pizza, pickle,
Pumpernickel,
My little guy
Shall have a tickle:

One for his nose,
And one for his toes,
And one for his tummy
Where the hot dog goes.

Dennis Lee

MY FATHER OWNS THE BUTCHER SHOP

My father owns the butcher shop,
My mother cuts the meat,
And I'm the little hot dog
That runs around the street.

Anonymous

RUNAWAY

I think today
I'll run away.
My heart is filled with sorrow.

I'll disappear
For one whole year,
Or else, come back tomorrow.

William Wise

SOMETIMES

Sometimes I simply have to cry,
I don't know why,
I don't know why.
There's really nothing very wrong,
I probably should sing a song
or run around and make some noise
or sit and tinker with my toys
or pop a couple of balloons
or play a game or watch cartoons,
but I'm feeling sad,
though I don't know why,
and all I want to do is cry.

Jack Prelutsky

IT'S ELEVEN O'CLOCK

It's eleven o'clock
and there's nothing to do
but stand on one leg
and then stand on two.

Eleven o'clock—
it's not a nice hour.
It's boring and hungry
and heavy and sour.

Nancy Chambers

SOMEONE'S FACE

Someone's face was all frowned shut,
   All squeezed full of grims and crinkles,
Pouts and scowls and gloomers, but
   I could see behind the wrinkles—

Even with her face a-twist,
   I saw Someone peeking through.
And when Someone's nose was kissed,
   Guess who came out giggling?—YOU!

John Ciardi

ROBERT, WHO IS OFTEN A STRANGER TO HIMSELF

Do you ever look in the looking-glass
And see a stranger there?
A child you know and do not know,
Wearing what you wear?

Gwendolyn Brooks

TEN FINGERS

I have ten little fingers
And they all belong to me.
I can make them do things.
Would you like to see?
I can shut them up tight
Or open them wide.
I can put them together
Or make them all hide.
I can make them jump high,
I can make them jump low,
I can fold them quietly
And hold them just so.

Anonymous

WIDE AWAKE

I have to jump up
  out of bed
  and stretch my hands
  and rub my head,
  and curl my toes
  and yawn
  and shake
  myself
  all wide-awake!

Myra Cohn Livingston

HERE ALL WE SEE

Here all we see
Is Ann's small nose,
A smile, two legs,
And ten pink toes,
Neatly arranged
In two short rows.

Walter de la Mare

SOMERSAULTS

It's fun turning somersaults
and bouncing on the bed,
I walk on my hands
and I stand on my head.

I swing like a monkey
and I tumble and I shake,
I stretch and I bend,
but I never never break.

I wiggle like a worm
and I wriggle like an eel,
I hop like a rabbit
and I flop like a seal.

I leap like a frog
and I jump like a flea,
there must be rubber
inside of me.

Jack Prelutsky

EARS HEAR

Flies buzz,
Motors roar.
Kettles hiss,
People snore.
Dogs bark,
Birds cheep.
Autos honk: *Beep! Beep!*

Winds sigh,
Shoes squeak.
Trucks honk,
Floors creak.
Whistles toot,
Bells clang.
Doors slam: *Bang! Bang!*

Kids shout,
Clocks ding.
Babies cry,
Phones ring.
Balls bounce,
Spoons drop.
People scream: *Stop! Stop!*

Lucia and James L. Hymes, Jr.

84

SNEEZE

There's a
sort of a
tickle
the size of a
nickel,
a bit like the
prickle
of sweet-sour
pickle;

it's a
quivery
shiver
the shape of a
sliver,
like eels in a
river;

a kind of a
wiggle
that starts as a
jiggle
and joggles
its way to a
tease,

which I
cannot
suppress
any longer,
I guess,
so pardon me,
please,
while I
sneeze.

Maxine Kumin

DRINKING FOUNTAIN

When I climb up
To get a drink,
It doesn't work
The way you'd think.

I turn it up,
The water goes
And hits me right
Upon the nose.

I turn it down
To make it small
And don't get any
Drink at all.

Marchette Chute

CRAYONS

I've colored a picture with crayons.
   I'm not very pleased with the sun.
I'd like it much stronger and brighter
   And more like the actual one.
I've tried with the crayon that's yellow,
   I've tried with the crayon that's red.
But none of it looks like the sunlight
   I carry around in my head.

Marchette Chute

KEZIAH

I have a secret place to go.
Not anyone may know.

And sometimes when the wind is rough
I cannot get there fast enough.

And sometimes when my mother
Is scolding my big brother,

My secret place, it seems to me,
Is quite the only place to be.

Gwendolyn Brooks

86

THE EVENING IS COMING

The evening is coming.
The sun sinks to rest.
The birds are all flying
straight home to their nests.
"Caw, caw," says the crow
as he flies overhead.
It's time little children
were going to bed.

Here comes the pony.
His work is all done.
Down through the meadow
he takes a good run.
Up go his heels,
and down goes his head.
It's time little children
were going to bed.

Anonymous

SILVERLY

Silverly,
    Silverly,
Over the
    Trees
The moon drifts
    By on a
Runaway
    Breeze.

Dozily,
    Dozily,
Deep in her
    Bed,
A little girl
    Dreams with the
Moon in her
    Head.

Dennis Lee

HUSHABYE MY DARLING

Hushabye my darling
Don't you make a peep
Little creatures everywhere
Are settling down to sleep

Fishes in the millpond
Goslings in the barn
Kitten by the fireside
Baby in my arms

Listen to the raindrops
Singing you to sleep
Hushabye my darling
Don't you make a peep

Clyde Watson

GOOD NIGHT, GOOD NIGHT

The dark is dreaming.
  Day is done.
Good night, good night
  To everyone.

Good night to the birds,
  And the fish in the sea,
Good night to the bears
  And good night to me.

Dennis Lee

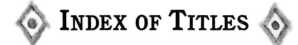

◆ INDEX OF TITLES ◆

◉ INDEX OF FIRST LINES ◉

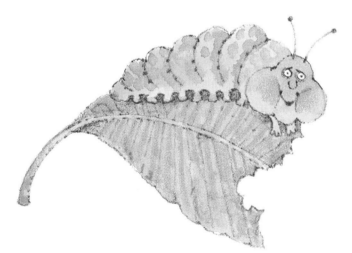

INDEX OF AUTHORS

⦿ ACKNOWLEDGMENTS ⦿

Every effort has been made to trace the ownership of all copyrighted material and to secure the necessary permissions to reprint these selections. In the event of any question arising as to the use of any material, the editor and publisher, while expressing regret for any inadvertent error, will be happy to make the necessary correction in future printings.

Grateful acknowledgment is made to the following for permission to reprint and/or record the copyrighted material listed below:

Abingdon Press for "Singing in the Spring" from CHERRY STONES! GARDEN SWINGS! by Ivy O. Eastwick. Copyright © 1962 by Abingdon Press. Used by permission. "Ten to One" and "The Puppy Chased the Sunbeam" from I RODE THE BLACK HORSE FAR AWAY by Ivy O. Eastwick. Copyright © 1960 by Abingdon Press. Used by permission.

Addison-Wesley Publishing Company, Inc., for "Ears Hear" from OODLES OF NOODLES by Lucia M. and James L. Hymes, Jr. Copyright © 1964 by Lucia M. and James L. Hymes, Jr. "Grasshopper Green" and "Makers" from BLUEBERRIES LAVENDER by Nancy Dingman Watson. Copyright © 1977 by Nancy Dingman Watson. Reprinted by permission of Addison-Wesley Publishing Company, Inc.

Atheneum Publishers, Inc., for "Cats and Dogs" from SNOWMAN SNIFFLES by N.M. Bodecker. Copyright © 1983 by N.M. Bodecker. A Margaret K. McElderry Book. "My Dragon" from THE PHANTOM ICE CREAM MAN: MORE NONSENSE POEMS by X.J. Kennedy. Copyright © 1979 by X.J. Kennedy. A Margaret McElderry Book. "Ants Live Here" and "Dragon Smoke" from I FEEL THE SAME WAY. Copyright © 1967 by Lilian Moore. "Bedtime Story" from SOMETHING NEW BEGINS by Lilian Moore. Copyright © 1982 by Lilian Moore. "Night Fun" from IF I WERE IN CHARGE OF THE WORLD by Judith Viorst. Copyright © 1981 by Judith Viorst. Reprinted with the permission of Atheneum Publishers, Inc.

Patricia Ayres for "Toaster Time" from THERE IS NO RHYME FOR SILVER by Eve Merriam. Published by Atheneum Publishers, Inc. Copyright © 1962 by Eve Merriam. Reprinted by permission of the author. All rights reserved.

Kenneth C. Bennett for "When You Talk to a Monkey" and "A Modern Dragon" by Rowena Bennett.

Curtis Brown, Ltd., for "Sneeze" from NO ONE WRITING A LETTER TO A SNAIL by Maxine W. Kumin. Copyright © 1962 by Maxine W. Kumin. "The Swallow" by Ogden Nash from THE NEW NUTCRACKER SUITE AND OTHER INNOCENT VERSES by Ogden Nash. Copyright © 1961, 1962 by Ogden Nash. Reprinted by permission of Curtis Brown, Ltd.

The Caxton Printers Ltd. for "Before the Monkey's Cage" from PICK-POCKET SONGS by Edna Becker. The Caxton Printers Ltd., Caldwell, Idaho. Used by permission.

Laura Cecil for "Run a Little" from THE BLACKBIRD IN THE LILAC by James Reeves. Copyright 1952 by James Reeves. Published by the Oxford University Press. Permission granted by the author's estate.

Marchette Chute for "Drinking Fountain" from AROUND AND ABOUT by Marchette Chute. Copyright © 1957 (E.P. Dutton), renewed 1985. Reprinted by permission of the author.

Lucille Clifton for "April" from EVERETT ANDERSON'S YEAR. Copyright © 1974 by Lucille Clifton. Reprinted by permission of Henry Holt and Company.

William Cole for "Two Sad" by William Cole. Copyright © 1977 by William Cole.

Delacorte Press for "The Toaster" from LAUGHING TIME by William Jay Smith. Copyright © 1953, 1955, 1956, 1957, 1959, 1968, 1974, 1977, 1980 by William Jay Smith. Reprinted by permission of Delacorte Press/Seymour Lawrence. A Merloyd Lawrence Book.

Doubleday & Company, Inc., for "Picnic Day" from A LITTLE BOX OF DAYS by Rachel Field. Copyright 1927 by Doubleday & Company, Inc. "I'd Like to Be a Lighthouse" from TAXIS AND TOADSTOOLS by Rachel Field. Copyright 1926 by Doubleday & Company, Inc. "December" from GAY GO UP by Rose Fyleman. Copyright 1929, 1930 by Doubleday & Company, Inc. Reprinted by permission of the publisher. Canadian rights administered by The Society of Authors.

E.P. Dutton, Inc., for "Icy" and "Under the Ground" from STORIES TO BEGIN ON by Rhoda W. Bacmeister. Copyright 1940 by E.P. Dutton, Inc., renewed 1968 by Rhoda W. Bacmeister. "Jump or Jiggle" by Evelyn Beyer from ANOTHER HERE AND NOW STORYBOOK by Lucy Sprague Mitchell. Copyright 1937 by E.P. Dutton, Inc., renewed 1965 by Lucy Sprague Mitchell. "Crayons," "My Teddy Bear," "Showers," and "Sleeping Outdoors" from RHYMES ABOUT US by Marchette Chute, Copyright © 1974 by Marchette Chute. "Woodpecker in Disguise" from BIRD IN THE BUSH by Grace Taber Hallock. Copyright 1930 by E.P. Dutton, Inc., renewed 1958 by Grace Taber Hallock. "The More It Snows" from THE HOUSE AT POOH CORNER by A.A. Milne, Copyright 1928 by E.P. Dutton, Inc., renewed 1956 by A.A. Milne. "Halfway Down" from WHEN WE WERE VERY YOUNG by A.A. Milne, Copyright 1924 by E.P. Dutton, Inc., renewed 1952 by A.A. Milne. Canadian rights administered by McClellan and Stewart Limited, Toronto. "The Snail and the Mouse" from I HAVE A SONG TO SING TO YOU by Laura E. Richards. Copyright 1938 by D. Appleton-Century Co., Inc. A Hawthorn Book. Reprinted by permission of E.P. Dutton, Inc., a division of New American Library.

Aileen Fisher for "Open House," "Pussy Willows," and "Snail's Pace" from IN THE WOODS, IN THE MEADOW, IN THE SKY by Aileen Fisher. Charles Scribner's Sons, 1965. By permission of the author.

Harcourt Brace Jovanovich, Inc., for "We Built a Castle Near the Rocks" from MORNING IS A LITTLE CHILD by Joan Walsh Anglund.

Harper & Row, Publishers, Inc., for "First Snow," "Five Years Old," and "The Mitten Song" from A POCKETFUL OF POEMS by Marie Louise Allen. Copyright 1939 by Harper & Row, Publishers, Inc., renewed 1956 by Merle Marston Garthwaite. "Keziah" and "Robert, Who Is Often a Stranger to Himself" from BRONZEVILLE BOYS AND GIRLS by Gwendolyn Brooks. Copyright © 1956 by Gwendolyn Brooks Blakely. "Someone's Face" from THE MAN WHO SANG THE SILLIES by John Ciardi (J.B. Lippincott Co.). Copyright © 1961 by John Ciardi. "Wouldn't You?" from YOU READ TO ME, I'LL READ TO YOU by John Ciardi (J.B. Lippincott Co.). Copyright © 1961 by John Ciardi. "Bedtime" and "Moon-Come-Out" from ELEANOR FARJEON'S POEMS FOR CHILDREN (J.B. Lippincott Co.) by Eleanor Farjeon. "Fairies" from ELEANOR FARJEON'S POEMS FOR CHILDREN (J.B. Lippincott Co.) by Eleanor Farjeon. Copyright 1926, 1954 by Eleanor Farjeon. "But I Wonder . . ." from OUT IN THE DARK AND DAYLIGHT: POEMS BY AILEEN FISHER. Copyright © 1980 by Aileen Fisher. "Raindrops" from OUT IN THE DARK AND DAYLIGHT: POEMS BY AILEEN FISHER. Copyright © 1966 by Aileen Fisher. "At Night" from OUT IN THE DARK AND DAYLIGHT: POEMS BY AILEEN FISHER. Copyright © 1973 by Aileen Fisher. "Wings" and "On Halloween" from OUT IN THE DARK AND DAYLIGHT: POEMS BY AILEEN FISHER. Copyright © 1980 by Aileen Fisher. "Peter and Wendy" from BREAD AN' JAM by Wymond Garthwaite. Copyright 1928 by Harper